Follow the Trail

Which line leads the sheepdog to the black sheep?

Follow the Trail: c

a.
b.
c.

Chicken Coop

Draw a chicken in the coop.

Odd One Out

Which of these isn't grown on a farm?

Answer: c

a.

b.

c.

d.

Decorate
the Scene

Decorate the farm scene below. You can use crayons and stickers.

Spot the
Difference

Can you spot the five differences between the two horses?

a.
.... carrots

c.
.... potatoes

How
Many?

The farmer has grown these vegetables.
Can you count how many vegetables there are?

Answer: a) 5, b) 3, c) 6, d) 4

b.
.... onions

.... lettuce

d.

Follow the Path

Show the farmer how to plough the field by following the dotted line.

Right or Wrong

Look at these animals and circle the ones that are shaded correctly.

a.

Name the Animals

Do you know the names of the farm animals? Follow the dotted lines to complete the words.

p i g

sheep

c o w

b.

a.

See the Spots

Circle the two pigs that have the same number of spots.

Can you draw eyes, beaks and legs onto the chicks?

Complete the **Chicks**

Save the **Crops!**

The farmer's lettuce is being eaten by the birds. Draw another scarecrow to help stop them!

Make a **Chick**

You will need: Paper Plate, Paper,
Yellow Poster Paint, Pens

1. Paint a paper plate yellow.
2. Make two yellow handprints on paper and ask
   an adult to cut them out.
3. Glue them behind the plate
   to make the chick's wings.
4. Draw on two eyes and a beak.

What's that Noise?

a. **Quack**

b. **Miaow**

c. **Oink**

d. **Moo**

h.

Match the animal to the noise it makes by drawing a line between them.

e.

g.

f.

New Shoes!

The horse needs new shoes. Can you find four that match?

d.

p.

o.

a.

e.

h.

l.

m.

f.

k.

b.

c.

i.

n.

g.

j.

Muddy Pig

Use a brown crayon to show how the pigs look after they've rolled around in the mud.

Slot the characters and bases together as shown, using the large bases for the Barn, Tractor and Cow.

Matching Cows

Shade the cow so it matches the cow below.

Make a Pig

You will need: Cardboard Tube, Sheet of Card, Scissors, Pink Poster Paint, Paintbrush, Glue

1. Paint a cardboard tube pink.
2. Paint a pig's face, two arms, two feet and a tail onto the card. Leave to dry.
3. Ask an adult to cut out all the pieces.
4. Glue them onto the cardboard tube.

Lost Sheep!

Farmer John has lost one of his sheep. Draw a line through the maze to help him find it.

the Big Picture

Find all the things listed below. Decorate the white paw print when you've found them.

4 chickens

3 cows

1 tractor

1 mouse

2 sheep

Match
the Shapes

Match each object to its shape by drawing a line between them.

a.

1.

2.

b.

c.

3.

4.

d.

Spot the Difference

Can you see the four differences between these two pictures?

How Many?

How many different shades are there in each picture? Write the correct numbers in the boxes.

a.

b.

c.

Answer: a = 5, b = 3, c = 3

Hidden Picture

Using the numbers below, decorate this picture to discover who is hiding.

1 = red
2 = orange
3 = yellow
4 = black
5 = blue

Test your Memory

Look at the pictures on the tray. When you can remember them all, turn the page.

Who is Mother?

How many yellow chicks are there?
Which hen is their mother.?

a.
b.
c.
d.
e.

How Many?

Help Farmer John count
all his animals.

1.  = ... chickens

2.  = ... pigs

3. = ... cows

Test your Memory

Can you see how many pictures have changed?
Do you remember how many blue things there were?
How many red things are there now?

Odd One Out

Count the number of pictures on each plate and write that number in the circle.

Which is the odd one out?

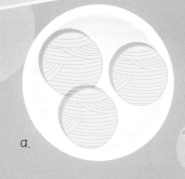

a.

. . . . . . cookies

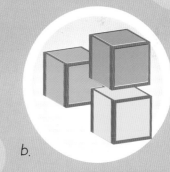

b.

. . . . . . building blocks

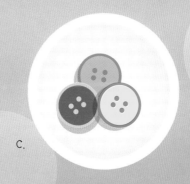

c.

. . . . . buttons

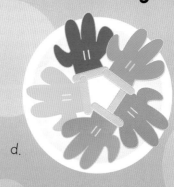

d.

. . . . . . gloves

Lots of Legs!

Count the legs on the animals and match them to the correct number.

Answer: a=8, b=2, c=4

a.

b.

c.

4

8

2

2 elephants

5 monkeys

2 penguins

Bat Cave

Bats are very shy and like to hide in dark caves. How many can you see?

Animal Escape!

These animals are on their way to the safari park, but some have escaped!
Count the animals to see which carriages have the wrong number of animals.
Draw in the missing animals to help the keeper.

4 giraffes

3 lions

Complete the Picture

Follow the instructions to finish the picture.

Draw 1 kite for the girl to fly.

Draw 8 apples on the tree.

Draw 6 flowers on the grass.

Draw 2 birds in the sky.

Draw 1 boy in the balloon.

Draw 3 cars on the road.

Join the Stars

The silver stars make a shape in the sky.
Connect the numbers to see what it is.

15
14   16
13   17
              18

            1   20
12   19
11

10
9
6

8
7   5
        4

    2
3

Making Monsters!

You have just discovered friendly
monsters in outer space and
you are the only person who has seen them!
Complete these monsters to show your
friends what the monsters look like.

Add 3 legs and 4 eyes to this monster.

3 , 2 , 1
Blast Off!

Follow the path of each space
rocket to find out which one
reaches the moon.

Answer: b

a)

b)

c)

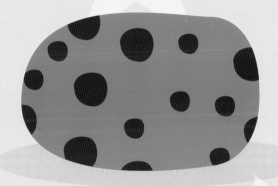

Add 8 legs, 3 heads,
10 eyes and 1 tail to
this monster.

Add 6 legs, 2 heads and
7 eyes to this monster.

Number Fun

Can you count to 10?
Fill in the numbers.

.... houses

.... cats

.... kite

1

2

3

4

5

.... flowers

.... boats

How **Many?**

a. How many sails are there on the boats? ....
b. How many windows are in the houses? ....
c. How many blue bows are on the kite? ....
d. How many red apples are there? ....

.... apples

.... frogs

6 7 8 9 10

.... shoes

.... spiders

.... balloons

Drawing Fun

Use your crayons and stickers to decorate the pictures.

Number Maze

Follow the numbers from 1 to 7 to find your way home through the town.

1

2

3

4

5

6

7

Flower Bed

Some of these flowers have petals missing. Add the correct number of petals to finish them.

6   5   10   8   7

Large tree
base

Slot the characters
and bases together
as shown below.

Large tree

Small tree base

Small tree

Whose House?

Draw a line to match the animals to their homes.

Answer: a+h, b+e, c+g, d+f

a. cat

b. bird

c. dog

d. horse

e.

f.

g.

h.

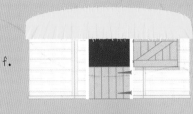

Fish Tank Fun!

Complete the fish tank.
Add some of the things listed below.

plants

stones

castle

fish

crab

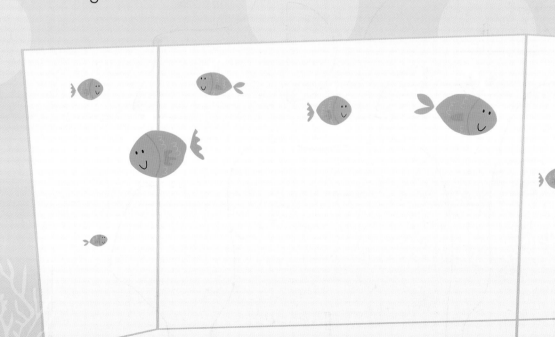

Match the Opposites

Draw lines to join the opposites.

cold

big

small

long

hard

soft

short

hot

Shade the Ships

Fill in the shapes to show what the picture is.

a = red, b = blue, c = orange, d = black, e = yellow

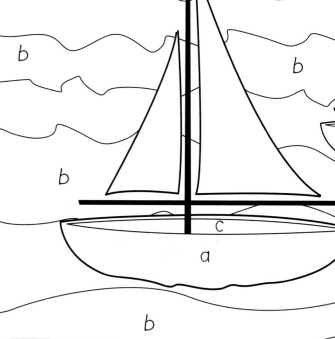

b
b
b
b
b
b
c
a
b

Match the Animals

Can you see which shadow and which word belongs to each animal?

cat

3.

bee

Answer: cat 1=e, dog=2+g, bee=4+f, duck=3+h

duck

f.

2.

1.

dog

4.

h.

Fill the Blanks

Complete each sentence choosing the correct word from the list. Use the pictures to help you.

Answer: a=kite, b=bike, c=dinner, d=mouse

b

a. The boy is flying a ....

b

b. The girl is riding her ....

e

c

c. The dog is eating his ....

b

d. The cat is chasing a ....

e

| kite | bike | dinner | mouse |

Under the Ocean

seahorse

turtle

seaweed

coral

crab

dolphin

What can you see under the ocean?
Circle the names on the right
when you find all the pictures.

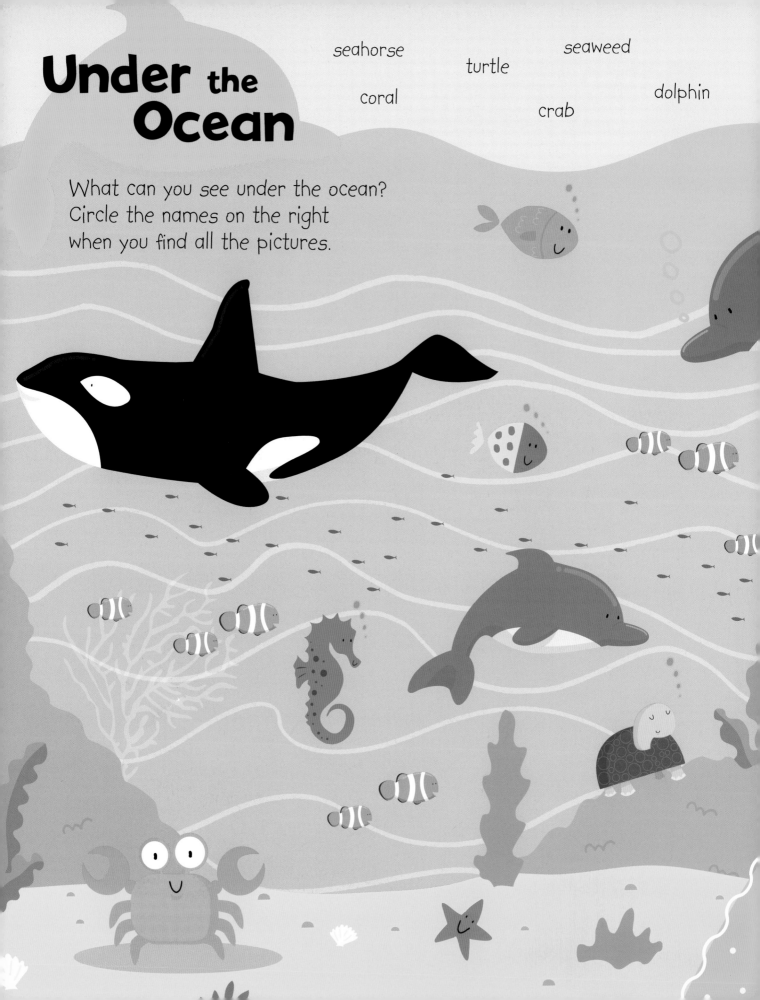

starfish

fish

Surfs Up!

The surfer has a new surfboard! Help decorate his surfboard with flowers, stripes, stars or circles. You can use stickers, too.

On the Beach

Decorate all the beach pictures with the correct shade.

orange towel

pink ice cream

green bucket

yellow sun hat

red ball

Match Up

Match the pictures that belong together by drawing a line between them.

cup

flowers

parrot

saucer

feather

vase

ball

boot

Hidden Letters

Can you find all the hidden letters in the flower garden? Circle them when you spot them. What word do they spell?

Answer: flowers

Buzzy Bees!

Follow the lines to show the bees the way home to their hive.

Pairs

Match the animal to the correct sentence by drawing a line between them.

a.

b.

c.

d.

1. I swing across the treetops.

2. I have over 60 teeth.

3. I can be poisonous.

4. I can learn to copy what you say!

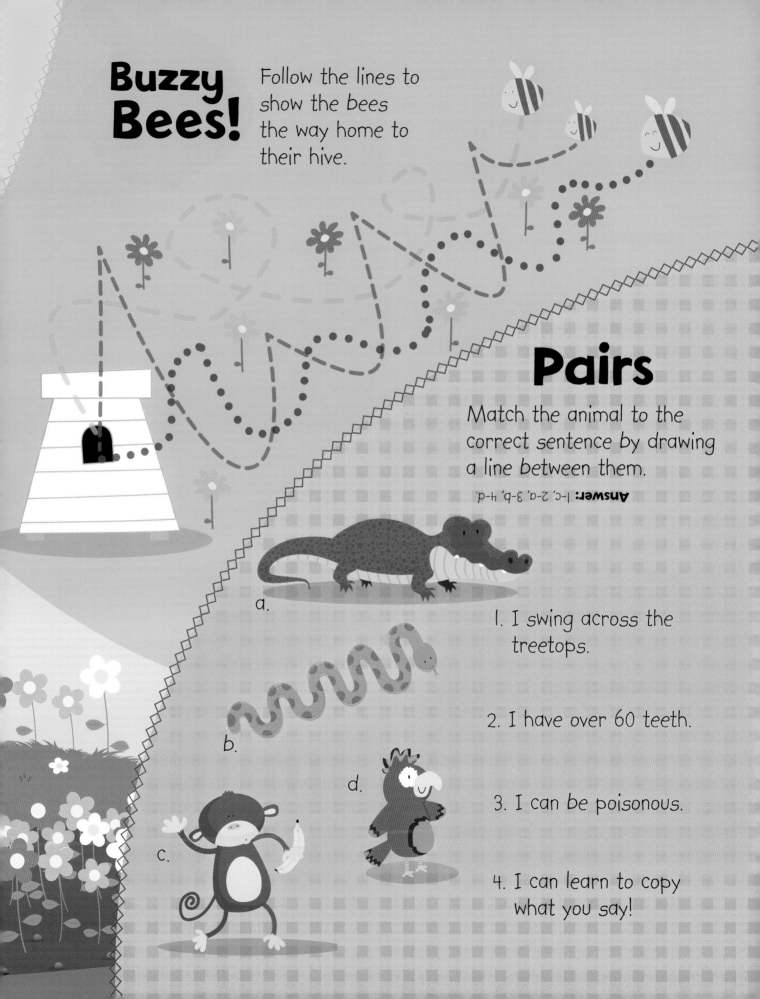

Going Away

You are going away.
How will you get where you're going?
Can you name the different ways
that you might travel?

Answer: a=ship, b=train, c=plane, d=car, e=bus

a.

b.

c.

e.

d.

....

....

....

....

....

Building
Blocks

Draw a city, using the shapes below.

square   rectangle   triangle   circle

Pack the Suitcase

What would you need for a trip to the South Pole to visit penguins? Draw lines between the pictures and the suitcase.

Answer: a, c, e, f, g.

a.

b.

c.

d.

e.

f.

g.

h.

Party Train

The train has five carriages full of party food and gifts. Using the list of words opposite, can you label the carriages to show what they're carrying?

Answer: a=hats, b=cake, c=ice cream, d=balloons, e=gifts

a.

b.

c.

d.

Balloons

The clown is bringing some balloons to the party. Can you match the words to the balloons?

----------   ----------   ----------

----------   ----------   ----------   ----------

----------   ----------   ----------

| red | yellow | blue | green | pink | orange | purple |

hats | balloons | cake | ice cream | gifts

Odd One Out

Can you see which is the odd one out in each group? Circle it.

Answer: Group 1 is d, Group 2 is g, Group 3 is p

Group 1

a.
b.
c.
d.
e.

Group 2

f.
g.
h.
i.
j.

Group 3

k.
l.
m.
n.
o.
p.

Match the Words

Draw a line between the words that are the same as the pictures.

bottle
spoon
fork
paper
soap
brush
cup

fork
cup
soap
bottle
brush
paper
spoon

Yes or No?

Can you answer these questions using 'yes' or 'no'?

1. Do dogs roar? . . . .

2. Are bananas red? . . . . . .

3. Can bees fly? . . . . .

4. Do chickens quack? . . . .

5. Is the sun yellow? . . . .

6. Do rabbits have 2 ears? . . . . .

Find the Animals

Can you spot the dog, cat, rabbit, squirrel and mouse hiding in the picture?

Who Lives There?

Only four of these animals live in the jungle. Draw circles around them.

Answer: a, d, e, g

a.

b.

c.

d.

e.

f.

g.

Copy Cat Animal Game

You can have as many players as you want.
Each player chooses a sticker and puts it onto a coin,
as a counter. You will also need a dice.
1. Put the coins at Start.
2. Take turns to roll the dice and move your counter.
3. Follow the instructions on the circle where you land.
4. The first player to reach the End wins.

Start

Waddle like a penguin

Miaow like a cat

Slither like a snake

Trumpet like an elephant

Stand on one leg like a flamingo

Flutter like a butterfly

Cat Face

Complete the cat's face, adding
a nose, eyes, mouth and whiskers.

Spider Legs

This spider needs legs!
Can you add them?

End

Roar like a lion

Wink like an owl

Scratch like a monkey

Woof like a dog

Run like a zebra

Stalk like a tiger

Tickle like a spider

Squeak like a mouse

Stretch like a giraffe

Name the Animals

Do you know the names of these animals? Follow the dotted lines to complete the names.

ti g e r

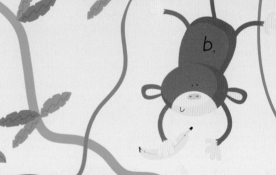

s n a k e

z e b r a

Silly Monkeys

Can you see the two monkeys that are the same?

Train Scene

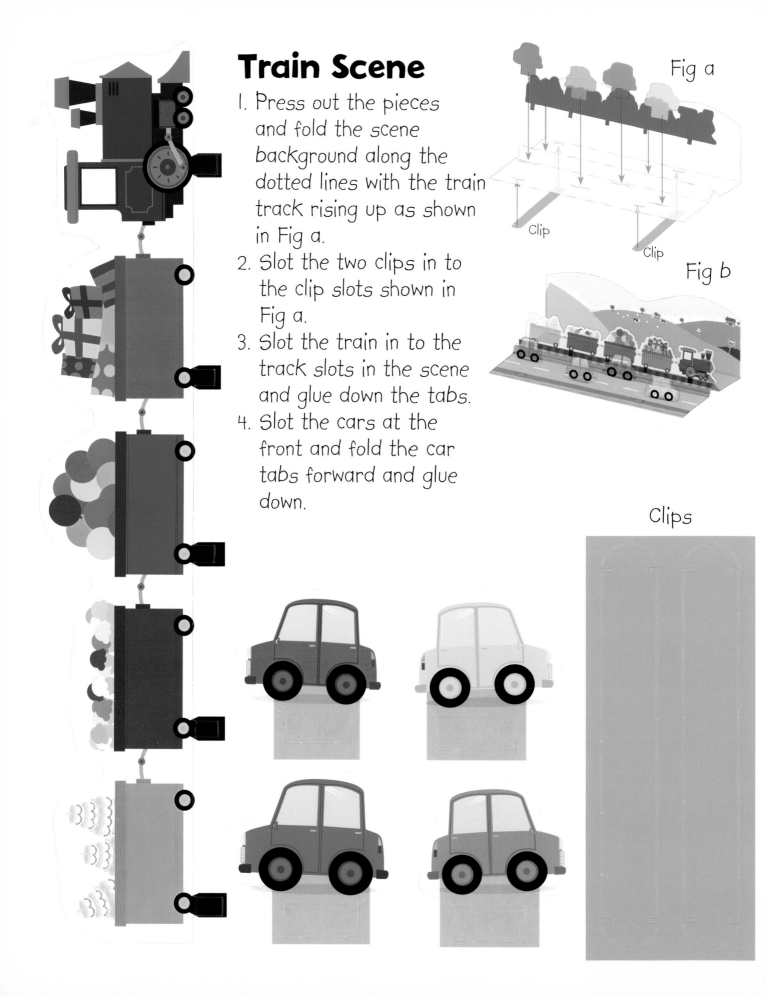

1. Press out the pieces and fold the scene background along the dotted lines with the train track rising up as shown in Fig a.
2. Slot the two clips in to the clip slots shown in Fig a.
3. Slot the train in to the track slots in the scene and glue down the tabs.
4. Slot the cars at the front and fold the car tabs forward and glue down.

Fig a

Clip

Clip

Fig b

Clips

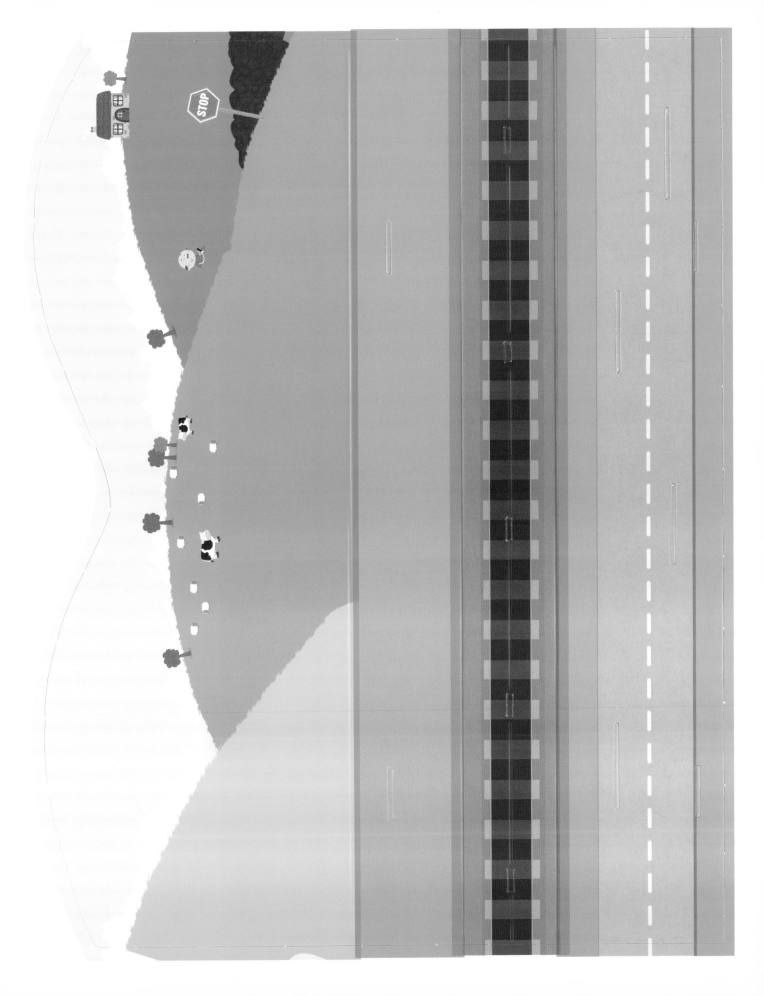

Handprint Lion Mane

You will need: Orange Poster Paint, Yellow Paper, Crayons, Scissors, Glue

1. Dip one hand in the paint.

2. Make lots of handprints in a circle.

3. When they are dry, ask an adult to cut out a yellow circle. Draw a lion's face on it and glue it in the middle of the handprints.

Spots and Stripes

These wild animals have lost their patterns. Can you help find them?

Answers: a-4, b-1, c-3, d-2

d. Zebra

c. Giraffe

b. Tiger

a. Leopard

4. Small Spots

3. Large spots

2. Black Stripes

1. Brown Stripes

Spot the Difference

There are five differences
between these two
crocodiles.
Can you spot them?

Pair up Penguins

Can you see which two
penguins on the ice are
the same?

b.

e.

a.

f.

c.

d.

Make a Killer Whale

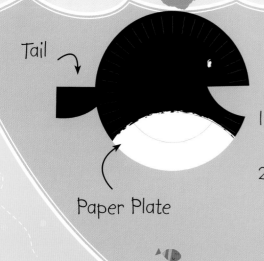

Tail

Paper Plate

You will need: Paper Plate, Glue, Black Poster Paint, Paintbrush, Scissors

1. Cut a small triangle out of the plate. This will be the mouth.
2. Glue it to the opposite side of the plate to make the tail. Paint the plate so it's black and white. Dip your hand in blue paint and make a handprint. Cut out the handprint and glue it above the whale to make his water spout.

Draw
a Panda

Copy the picture of the panda, square by square, into the blank grid.

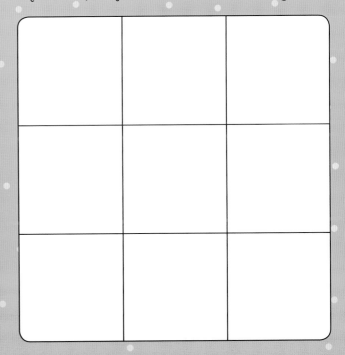

River Fun

How many animals can you spot in this river?
Write the number in the boxes.

There are   ducks

There are   fish

There are   frogs

There are   dragonflies

Match the Tracks

Dot-to-Dot

Connect the dots to see what animal
is running through the flowers.

Animals leave different prints.
Can you match the animals to their correct prints?

a.

b.

c.

d.

e.

1.

2.

3.

4.

5.

Whose Tail?

The animals are missing their tails.
Help put the right tail on the right body.

a.

b.

c.

d.

1.

2.

3.

4.

Opposites

Draw a line from each picture to its opposite.

C. COLD polar bear

a. SLOW tortoise

b. BIG elephant

f. HOT lizard

Find
the Bananas

Help the elephant find his way through the maze to the tasty bananas.

Guide

1 = red

2 = blue

3 = yellow

4 = purple

5 = green

d. FAST cheetah

e. SMALL mouse

Matching Shades

Draw a red line between the animals that live in the jungle, a green line for those living on a farm and a blue line for the animals living in the sea.

Answer: a–d, b–f, c–e

a.

b.

c.

d.

e.

f.

Decorate
the Butterfly

Use the numbers to decorate the butterfly using your crayons or felt tips.

Mixed - up Bodies

The front and back halves of the animals are mixed up. Can you match the correct fronts and backs?

Answer: a-d, b-e, f-g, c-h

f. e.

c.

d.

b. a.

g.

h.

Missing Piece

Can you find the missing piece to complete the puzzle? You can also cut out the puzzle and glue the pieces on to card. Cut out the pieces to have your own puzzle!

Answer: e

a.

b.

c.

d.

e.

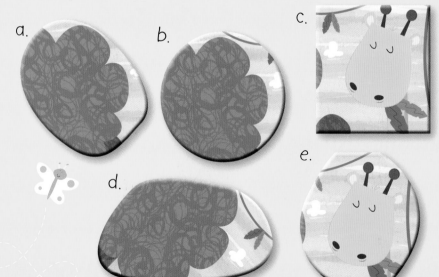